Wrapped *in* Wonder

JULIE RANSON

Contact Information: jjransonauthor@gmail.com

Cover art by Julie J. Ranson

Painted Pen Press, LLC, 7410 Hull Street Road, Ste 200, Unit #345, North Chesterfield, VA 23235

Publishing History First Edition, 2025

Trade Paperback ISBN 979-8-9990415-2-4

Digital ISBN 979-8-9990415-3-1

Published in the United States of America

Contents

Introduction

DON'T YOU JUST LOVE Christmas? *The day* is incredible for those of us who are kids are heart. While many denounce the appearance of Christmas decor alongside pumpkins and the warm colors of fall, anticipating the arrival of Jesus' birthday means busy days and building excitement. And though our childish dreams of perfectly decorated branches and glitter everywhere (okay, that might be just me), the chasing of Christmas excitement can overwhelm and tire us. How do we overcome the disappointment or exhaustion of the holiday season?

Advent spans the period of four Sundays and weeks before Christmas. Advent means coming or arrival. The Christian's current period of waiting, of course, is for the second coming of Jesus. Perhaps we can capture the true spirit of the season by focusing on patiently seeking Jesus. Waiting in anticipation, that's another meaning of advent. Those words seem incongruous, don't they? But who says we can't simultaneously slow down our minds and quicken our attention to the arrival of the newborn King?

My hope is that the daily readings in this devotional, *Wrapped in Wonder,* will guide your heart to a quiet, thoughtful place. I pray that your spiritual attention during each day of the Advent season will renew your focus on His blessed birth. Together, let's explore the well-known cast of characters (Mary, Joseph, Jesus, angels, shepherds) and themes of hope, peace, and love. Let's consider how we might incorporate all these stories and blessings into our days leading up to Christmas, and then the new year.

Each day, we'll focus on preparing ourselves during this waiting season. A focused prayer kicks off every seven days. The readings end with a sentence prayer and a few lines from beloved Christmas or Christian hymns. Below, you'll find a link to a playlist of the amazing music I've chosen.

Because the liturgical calendar celebrates the four Sundays before Christmas Day, those dates shift every year. So, I've arranged the daily readings to start on the first of December. After Christmas Day, you'll have six more readings, prayers, and songs that will focus your heart and mind on preparing for a new calendar year — an important time of reflection and planning for new things. I promise not to ask you about your resolutions!

May God bless our days together leading up to and beyond this holy season.

~Julie

Playlist Link: **tiny.cc/wrapped**

Week One Prayer & Scripture Reading

We search for God in the
most unexpected places —
as an infant born in hum-
ble surroundings, and in
the emptiness of a grave.
Grant us listening hearts,
O God, so we might recog-
nize your nearness during
this sacred time of celebration as we await the arrival
of Jesus Christ.
Amen.

This is how the birth of Jesus the Messiah came about: His mother Mary was pledged to be married to Joseph, but before they came together, she was found to be pregnant through the Holy Spirit. Because Joseph her husband was faithful to the law, and did not want to expose her to public disgrace, he had in mind to divorce her quietly. But after he had considered this, an angel of the Lord appeared to him in a dream and said, "Joseph son of David, do not be afraid to take Mary home as your wife, because what is conceived in her is from the Holy Spirit. She will give birth to a son, and you are to give him the name Jesus." (Matthew 1:18–21, NIV).

December 9

WHEN MY CHILDREN WERE young, our church invited four families to "perform" the Advent readings on the four Sundays leading up to Christmas. To be chosen to do this was both special and nerve-wracking. Not for me, but for the rest of the bunch in my house, oh my. Lighting the correct candles in the correct order, what a worry it was! It was velvet-dresses-and-tears time. We survived and grew from the experience.

Well, *I* grew spiritually from it. Unaware of the liturgical calendar most of my life, I was an adult before I intentionally observed the Advent period. I love this period of waiting — I understand I'm waiting for something special. And, no, it's not Santa Claus.

It's too easy to get caught up in the glitter and gifts of Christmas.

But the slow spiritual slide to Christmas that Advent affords keeps this believer's heart ready and focused on the true reason for the season.

We can all agree that we live in difficult times. Many of us have been tested in unbelievable ways — financially, spiritually, physically. We likely have been tempted to ask God for the same things the Psalmist asked:

God, take us back. Show us your kindness so we can be saved. (Psalm 80:3, NCV).

The Psalmist asks God to show His kindness — so we can be saved. Have you had to drink tears this year? I have — too many, I must say. But did you know that salt is good for the body? It helps with digestion and is good for the heart, to name just two salty benefits. Salt is essential, and it is salvation to the physical body.

It is the hope of salvation that keeps the believer on course, ready, and eternally faithful. His kindness is coming. His kindness is here.

Therefore, the Lord himself will give you a sign: The virgin will conceive and give birth to a son, and will call him Immanuel. (Isaiah 7:14, NCV)

Pray

Lord, teach me to wait with trust, knowing Your timing is perfect.
Amen.

Sing

Go Tell It On the Mountain
(African-American spiritual)
Down in a lowly manger
Our humble Christ was born,
And God sent us salvation
That blessed Christmas morn.
Go, tell it on the mountain,
Over the hills and everywhere;
Go, tell it on the mountain
That Jesus Christ is born.

December 2

THE FIRST CANDLE LIT on an Advent wreath is purple. It stands for hope. It has been called the Prophecy Candle because of the Old Testament prophets who foretold the Messiah's birth. Isaiah's may be the most memorable and most quoted prophecy, but many others got into the prophecy game. (Or should I more properly say, God used them to deliver messages to His people.)

'The days are coming,' declares the Lord, 'when I will fulfill the good promise I made to the people of Israel and Judah. In those days and at that time I will make a righteous Branch sprout from David's line; he will do what is just and right in the land. In those days Judah will be saved and Jerusalem will live in safety. This is the name by which will be called: The Lord Our Righteous Savior.' (Jeremiah 33:14–16, NIV).

Some days it is hard to be hopeful. When I was a caregiver, I lingered mostly in the hope of good days. As my husband's illness progressed, we expected that the bad days might outnumber better ones. We were thankful for his doctors and the extraordinary care we received from an incredible teaching hospital. Our gratitude, though, for the murmurings of Christian prayer warriors could not possibly be measured. Their prayers, along with our own faithful appeals, were the foundation of our hope.

I can't imagine the day-to-day manifestation of hopefulness in the Israelites. So disobedient, these people suffered at the hands of despicable rulers in and out of times of captivity. Yet, their faithful preachers and prophets touted a coming Messiah to restore the nation and the people.

You alone are the Lord. You made the heavens, even the highest heavens, and all their starry host, the earth and all that is on it, the seas and all that is in them. You give life to everything, and the multitudes of heaven worship you (Nehemiah 9:6, NIV).

God is a faithful provider. He proved this to the recalcitrant Israelites repeatedly. Nehemiah, for example, was an extremely successful leader. He led the Israelites as they came out of Babylonian exile. Aligned with God and His calling, Nehemiah overcame the odds and oversaw the rebuilding of the Jerusalem wall to protect God's people.

More hope!

Pray

God in Heaven, even in darkness, help me trust that the light is coming. Amen.

Sing

I Wonder as I Wander
(John Jacob Niles, 1933)
I wonder as I wander, out under the sky,
how Jesus the Savior did come for to die
for poor ordinary people like you and like I;
I wonder as I wander, out under the sky.

December 3

WHAT'S THE MOST SURPRISING thing that ever happened to you? Was it a total WOW? How did you feel? Perhaps my biggest personal surprise was when I received an outstanding faculty award at a community college. Even more surprising moments occurred when my children were honored for their performances in school or in sports.

Elizabeth and Zechariah experienced more than one amazing surprise before their son was even born. I urge you to read the entire first chapter of Luke, parts of which are quoted here.

But the angel said to him, "Zechariah, don't be afraid. God has heard your prayer. Your wife, Elizabeth, will give birth to a son, and you will name him John. He will bring you joy and gladness, and many people will be happy because of his birth" (Luke 1:12–14, NCV).

First, Zechariah was told that his long-barren wife would have a son. Though consistently obedient to God, Zechariah still questioned the angel's news, and thus, he became mute for a time. I wonder if he asked what took so long to have his prayers answered. Elizabeth lost the shame of her barrenness when she conceived a child at her advanced age.

Later, Zechariah's wife, Elizabeth, became pregnant and did not go out of her house for five months. Elizabeth said, "Look what the Lord has done for me! My people were ashamed of me, but now the Lord has taken away that shame" (Luke 1:24–25, NCV).

When an angel again visited Mary, he told her about Elizabeth. That same angel exclaimed, "God can do anything!" So, Mary went to visit her cousin Elizabeth to rejoice with her in this extraordinary news.

Elizabeth cried out in a loud voice, "God has blessed you more than any other woman, and He has blessed the baby to which you will give birth. Why has this good thing happened to me, that the mother of my Lord comes to me? When I heard your voice, the baby inside me jumped with joy" (Luke 1:42–44, NCV).

Though our current culture devalues life at every opportunity, we read here that the unborn baby John, in Elizabeth's womb, recognized the presence of the Son of God growing inside Mary.

I'd put that in the "total wow" category, wouldn't you?

Pray

Father, may my soul burn with holy anticipation in this season. Amen.

Sing

Come Thou Long Expected Jesus
(Charles Wesley, 1744)
Born thy people to deliver,
born a child and yet a King,
born to reign in us forever,
now thy gracious kingdom bring.

December 4

WHEN A WOMAN FINDS herself pregnant, it's usually a time of celebration. Both parents-to-be are ecstatic — a prayer's been answered, a gift awaits.

Thousands of years ago, a young woman named Mary was engaged to a hard-working man and found herself with child. She'd had a visit from the Lord, and she sang of it. A miracle was in the works.

The man, Joseph, heard this news and surely panicked. What terror might have plagued him? Can you imagine the fear — given the time and place, and their individual circumstances? The anticipation of their marriage faded quickly, no doubt. As a righteous man, he thought to make it all go away quietly to avoid embarrassing poor Mary.

God had other plans. Of course He did!

When Joseph woke up, he did what the angel of the Lord had commanded him and took Mary home as his wife. But he did not consummate their marriage until she gave birth to a son. And he gave him the name Jesus. (Matthew 1:24–25, NIV)

Even though none of this news made sense, Joseph trusted his Lord. He didn't consult friends or family. Joseph obeyed God and married Mary as he'd promised from the start. As we know from the biblical account of Jesus' birth (found only in Luke 2), he also obeyed man's law and went with Mary to Bethlehem for the government census. All of this obedience mattered.

We don't know much about Joseph — besides his faithfulness to God, that is. Joseph is a blip in Jesus' story, while Mary gets more mention in the New Testament telling of Jesus' life. But Joseph definitely factored in Jesus' development through childhood. We feel his influence.

Joseph was handed a significant responsibility — to be the earthly father of Jesus, the Son of God. He took his family to the temple, provided for his family, taught his sons — including Jesus — a trade.

What a magnificent measure of obedience to keep all those promises — to God, to Mary, his sons, and his community.

It makes this believer wonder where she might need to be more trusting and obedient. What about you?

Pray

Lord, help me obey even when I don't understand the path ahead.
Amen.

Sing

O Come, Emmanuel
(Unknown, 12th century)
O come, O come, Immanuel,
and ransom captive Israel
that mourns in lonely exile here
until the Son of God appear.

December 5

THIS IS HOW THE Christmas story unfolds in the Bible. The second chapter of the gospel of Luke is the only place we can read the details of Jesus' birth story — the one we all treasure in our hearts. Whether raised in a church or not, nearly everyone knows Jesus is the reason for the season. And while many focus only on that jolly old elf, still they have the origin story of Christmas in their heads, even if they don't hold Jesus in their hearts. You know why?

It's an incredible tale.

So Joseph also went up from the town of Nazareth in Galilee to Judea, to Bethlehem the town of David, because he belonged to the house and line of David. He went there to register with Mary, who was pledged to be married to him and was expecting a child (Luke 2: 4–5, NIV).

Engaged couple: Joseph, the carpenter, and Mary, the pregnant teen.

A long journey.

No rooms to be found.

Angels.

Shepherds.

And a prophecy fulfilled.

But you, Bethlehem Ephrathah, though you are small among the clans of Judah, out of you will come for me one who will be ruler over Israel, whose origins are from of old, from ancient times (Micah 5:2, NIV).

Advent is a precious and splendid time of anxious anticipation — the waiting is magical, isn't it? It means so much more than the world out there understands. And remaining alert to the approach of Christmas Day, we must contemplate the meaning of Jesus' birth and ministry. We know how this story ultimately ends and now wait patiently for His second coming. If that's not true for us today, it's time to get down on our knees in prayer and worship.

How are you going to spend the coming days? Why not share the entire incredible tale with someone?

Pray

Dear God, fill me with authentic faith as I await the celebration of Christ's coming. Amen.

Sing

O Little Town of Bethlehem
(Phillips Brooks, 1868)
O little town of Bethlehem, how still we see thee lie!
Above thy deep and dreamless sleep the silent stars go by.
Yet in thy dark streets shineth the everlasting light;
the hopes and fears of all the years are met in thee tonight.

December 6

I'VE GIVEN BIRTH TO three children — in hospitals — and cannot imagine doing it any other place. I often wonder what Mary expected of childbirth—what had the women in her family told her about it? Did she wonder if the birth of Jesus might go differently? He being the Son of God and all.

Granted, there were no hospitals, but surely she was taken aback (even disappointed) by the setting in which she gave birth to the Christ-child. Her surroundings were worse than primitive.

Then, shepherds arrive, bringing with them villagers who'd heard their story. Everyone was amazed, and it surely was crowded and noisy. Annoying, even. I remember clearly after my first child was born that I didn't want any visitors. Exhaustion and fear stalk a new mother like a lion.

So they hurried off and found Mary and Joseph, and the baby, who was lying in the manger. When they had seen him, they spread the word concerning what had been told them about this child, and all who heard it were amazed at what the shepherds said to them. But Mary treasured up all these things and pondered them in her heart. The shepherds returned, glorifying and praising God for all the things they had heard and seen, which were just as they had been told (Luke 2:16–20, NIV).

We don't know exactly how Mary felt in that moment other than what scripture says. *She pondered it in her heart.* She knew something cataclysmic was happening... the angel had told her the truth about the birth of God's son.

The circumstances of that birth might have seemed all wrong, but Mary knew in her heart it was all quite right. Mary loved and served God. She had faith. She believed in God's promises. As a young woman of faith, she too had prayed for the coming of the Messiah to save her people.

What a heady and overwhelming truth for a young woman to ponder. She had prayed, "Come, Emmanuel." Because of her faithfulness, the promised Messiah entered the world through her — *Emmanuel, God with us.*

All this took place to fulfill what the Lord had said through the prophet: "The virgin will conceive and give birth to a son, and they will call him Immanuel" (which means "God with us") (Matthew 1:22–23, NIV).

Will you say, Come, to Jesus today?

Pray

Let my heart be quick to respond to Your voice, Lord. Amen.

Sing

Away in a Manger
(Martin Luther, 1524)
Away in a manger, no crib for a bed,
the little Lord Jesus laid down His sweet head;
the stars in the heavens looked down where He lay,
the little Lord Jesus asleep on the hay.

December 7

HAVE YOU EVER BEEN given a special assignment? I remember my kids in their elementary school years being excited to be chosen as the teacher's messenger. They'd deliver the attendance report and other notes to the office — so important! I'm sure they felt shivers of giddiness to get to leave the classroom and fulfill an essential role.

Throughout the Old and New Testaments, the Bible offers a variety of angelic encounters, but the ones we think about, sing about, are most relevant in the Christmas story.

You're minding your own business and then... a light flickers and then it grows larger and larger overhead until it's practically blinding you. You look up, blinking.

An angel appears to share some terrific news. Following that astounding announcement, there's an overwhelming racket — angelic voices shouting praises to God.

When the angels had left them and gone into heaven, the shepherds said to one another, "Let's go to Bethlehem and see this thing that has happened, which the Lord has told us about." (Luke 2:15, NIV).

What would you do?

You head to town, that's what! A talking angel, singing voices, bright lights are certainly a recipe for excitement. And obedience. Remember, the angel told the shepherds this:

This will be a sign to you: You will find a baby wrapped in cloths and lying in a manger (Luke 2:12, NIV).

The command was clear: Go. Find.

The promise attached to the angel's urging is found throughout the Bible, and in the Old Testament we read:

You will seek me and find me when you seek me with all your heart (Jeremiah 29:13, NIV).

Eventually, the wise men turned up. And believers everywhere know... wise men still seek Him today.

Are you a seeker? Where will you look for Him today?

Pray

Dear Jesus, let my spirit rise with hope as I look for the light ahead. Amen.

Sing

Angels We Have Heard on High
(French carol, 1855)
Come to Bethlehem and see
Him whose birth the angels sing;
come, adore on bended knee
Christ the Lord, the newborn *King.*
Gloria, in excelsis Deo!
Gloria, in excelsis Deo!

Week Two Prayer & Scripture Reading

Dear God, when darkness surrounds me, I anchor myself in hope. Help me trust that Your light still shines, that tomorrow holds promise, and setbacks are temporary. Fill my heart with faith that guides me forward, knowing hope is never misplaced when rooted in You. Amen.

And Mary said: "My soul glorifies the Lord and my spirit rejoices in God my Savior, for he has been mindful of the humble state of his servant. From now on all generations will call me blessed, for the Mighty One has done great things for me—holy is his name" (Luke 1:46-49, NIV).

December 8

UNTIL I ATTENDED A Methodist church in adulthood, I knew nothing about the liturgical calendar. Thus, I'd never heard of Advent, which means "coming" in Latin. As a child, I certainly experienced the excitement and anticipation of Christmas, the coming of Santa Claus. Many Sunday School teachers shared the lessons about the birth of Jesus, but Christmas trees, silver tinsel hung one slinky strand at a time, gift wrap, and anticipation were pretty much my entire experience of Advent through many Decembers. I certainly don't remember humming, *Come, Thou Long-Expected Jesus.*

As it is written in the book of the words of Isaiah the prophet: A voice of one calling in the wilderness, "Prepare the way for the Lord, make straight paths for him. Every valley shall be filled in, every mountain and hill made low. The crooked roads shall become straight, the rough ways smooth. And all people will see God's salvation." (Luke 3:4–6, NIV).

The days leading up to Christmas are meant for preparation. Preparation of the heart, not the home. So many people, myself included, get caught up in the secular trappings of decorating, baking, and gift-buying—and everything else the world throws at us. The sparkle and the noise distract us.

And we forget to prepare our hearts.

But imagine, if you will, a prophet, John the Baptist, preaching about a ministry that's about to happen. It's just around the corner.

Jesus is going to appear on the ministerial scene finally. "Prepare the way of the Lord!" John the Baptist declared. He wasn't talking about paving a road. Or setting the scene just right. And John's words make me wonder...

How do we make room for Jesus 2,000 years later?

Like preparing to build a road or a theatre set, preparation is necessary to receive Jesus. God must prepare our hearts, and we must grant all the permits for that to happen. Unlock the door and let Him in. And maybe we'll get there when we stop focusing on the wrong stuff. Let's make this far less complicated, shall we? Will you join me and invite His light into your darkness?

In the Advent wreath, the second purple candle's flickering flame reminds us who Jesus truly is: "*In him was life, and that life was the light of all mankind. The light shines in the darkness, and the darkness has not overcome it.*" *(John 1:4–5, NIV).*

Let it shine in your darkness. Let the warm glow of the manger *banish* the darkness.

Pray

Draw me near, Lord, and awaken my heart with Your light. Amen.

Sing

O, Thou That Tellest
(G.F. Handel, 1741)
O thou that tellest good tidings to Zion
Arise, shine, for thy light is come
Arise, arise Arise, shine, for thy light is come
And the glory of the Lord The glory of the Lord
Is risen, Is risen Upon thee.

December 9

In Luke 1, Zechariah has an encounter with Gabriel, who tells the old man that he and his wife are going to have a son that they'll name John. Well past childbearing years, the couple are astounded by the news, but Zechariah doesn't seem to be surprised by the angelic presence. Mary also meets Gabriel, who tells her she's going to have a son (conceived of God) that she'll name Jesus. Now, I don't believe that people of that time were immune to surprise or accustomed to angelic visitations, but it sure is "funny" how these angelic appearances are taken rather in stride.

Perhaps, today, we're too dramatic.

Angels. What do you think about them? What do you imagine they look like? Does an angel look like Clarence in the movie It's a Wonderful Life? That sweet, bumbling fellow. Or are they majestic and awe-inspiring? I'm taking my cue from this third angelic visitation:

Suddenly a great company of the heavenly host appeared with the angel, praising God and saying, "Glory to God in the highest heaven, and on earth peace to those on whom his favor rests." (Luke 2:13-14, NIV).

Recently, I heard a radio host suggest that the heavenly host that appeared with the spokes-angel likely filled the sky left-to-right, up and down. Imagine that — the entire sky glistening with angelic bodies. Not that our human imagination could accurately conjure up the real thing, but we can sustain our imaginations with the images many famous artists have given us, varied that they are.

Maybe you've not thought much of the angels that linger around Earth. They're here, you know. If Satan has his team of demons thwarting God's work (we always believe those exist, don't we?), then why not consider that angels are looking out for opportunities to help us?

An angel visited Balaam, and here's what happened. *The Lord opened Balaam's eyes, and he saw the angel of the Lord standing in the road with his sword drawn. So he bowed low and fell facedown (Numbers 22:31, NIV).*

Here's what we know from illustrations in scripture: Balaam was awestruck; the shepherds were terrified. And remember the admonition in Hebrews 13:2, that you may entertain angels without knowing it.

How would you react if an angel visited you? Or has one already made you aware of its presence?

Pray

I long for You, Lord—stir my soul with excitement for Your nearness.
Amen.

Sing

Angels From the Realms of Glory
(James Montgomery, 1816)
Angels from the realms of glory, wing your flight o'er all the earth;
ye who sang creation's story now proclaim Messiah's birth:
Come and worship, come and worship, worship Christ, the newborn
king.

December 10

Why did God choose shepherds for His communication team? It's an important question. The Pharisees, the religious leaders of the day, were on the lookout for the promised Messiah. Why wouldn't they be the ones to first hear the news the Messiah's birth and carry it to the people? As religious leaders, they were already in the perfect position to share this kind of information.

In *Mere Christianity (page 53)*, C.S. Lewis wrote, *God has landed on this enemy-occupied world in human form.*

Alas, God sent angels to the fields to tell the shepherds about this fulfillment of prophecy. This makes sense in light of the entire history of God's work with His creation, humankind. God uses the humbled, the hurting.

He uses the *unlikely.*

And there were shepherds living out in the fields nearby, keeping watch over their flocks at night. An angel of the Lord appeared to them, and the glory of the Lord shone around them, and they were terrified. But the angel said to them, "Do not be afraid. I bring you good news that will cause great joy for all the people. Today in the town of David a Savior has been born to you; he is the Messiah, the Lord. This will be a sign to you: You will find a baby wrapped in cloths and lying in a manger." (Luke 2:8–12, NIV).

Think about it. The shepherds were far less likely to question the news. You know, analyze and study it to death, like the educated Pharisees would have done. Instead, the shepherds left their sheep immediately to find this amazing baby—Jesus, the Son of God.

Jesus' arrival as a baby was also unlikely in the expectations of that day's leaders. They were waiting for a military leader and king! We are too—King Jesus. Jesus had to be born because when they sinned, Adam and Eve failed in their role as image-bearers of God. Jesus was and is the perfect bearer of God's image. He was the fix—the solution—to the problem of human sin. His shed blood makes us beautiful in God's eyes.

What is your mind focused on today? Why not spend time pondering the unlikely quality of that birthday night long ago and what that means for your life and salvation.

Pray

Father, as I wait, fill my heart with faith instead of fear. Amen.

Sing

While Shepherds Watched Their Flocks
(Tate, 1700)
While shepherds watched their flocks by night,
all seated on the ground
an angel of the Lord came down, and glory shone around.
"Fear not," said he for mighty dread had seized their troubled mind
"glad tidings of great joy I bring to you and all mankind."

December 11

THE ANGEL WHO APPEARED to the shepherds ushers us into the light and joy of the Good News of the Gospel.

But the angel said to them, "Do not be afraid. I bring you good news that will cause great joy for all the people." (Luke 2:10, NIV).

I can just imagine the shepherds whooping and hollering upon hearing this news and seeing this unusual sight. You see, they were part of the canceled culture of their time — unclean, not trusted, lowest of the low. This paranormal event must have heightened all of their senses that starry night. Did the hair on the back of their necks prickle?

It's a lot to ponder. Too much and too hard to understand. But we don't have to understand it all.

God entrusted *them* with the important announcement of Jesus' birth! And they rushed to see the miracle; they did not wait.

This period *of waiting* invites us into the joy of knowing Jesus. Here is our opportunity to have a relationship with God.

Waiting. That's what we are doing in the days before Christmas. It's not that hard, is it? We can fill our waiting minutes with decorating, baking, and visiting family and friends. The holiday season flies — though probably moreso for the grownups than the children waiting for the visit of that Jolly Old Elf.

We spend a lot of our lifetimes in waiting mode, don't we?

In our get-it-in-an-instant culture, anticipation is not as exciting as I remember it *back in the day.* I had to wait to get my driver's license

— I was 16 1/2, for heaven's sake! I stood by the mailbox anxiously awaiting news of all kinds — scholarships, college acceptance, a letter from a cute boy in Virginia. That certainly paints a more stirring scene than sitting and staring at one's email inbox.

Adults should be better at waiting than their younger selves, but we rarely succeed. We hit "refresh" on the medical portal for test results. We check our mobile phone for that oh-so-important message. Or we rush out to buy some item we must have—now.

Waiting itself isn't bad for us. It's our behavior that matters most. Letting anxiety cloud our hearts and minds is not the path to peace. It's not the music of a faithful soul, either.

Pray

Father, let Your peace guard my heart and mind in Christ Jesus. Amen.

Sing

The First Noel
(English carol, 16th century)
The First Noel the angel did say
Was to certain poor shepherds in fields as they lay;
In fields as they lay, keeping their sheep,
On a cold winter's night that was so deep.
Noel, Noel, Noel, Noel,
Born is the King of Israel.

December 12

Happiness can be a fleeting thing. One minute you're happy, the next moment you're not because of *some thing*. Your life is acted upon and suddenly your happiness is gone.

Joy and happiness are not the same. Joy is not dependent on circumstances. Even in our darkest hour, when happiness has fled, He will redeem the moment. Joy can fill us and envelop our hearts — just like how the shepherds felt that awe-filled night.

Though you have not seen him, you love him; and even though you do not see him now, you believe in him and are filled with an inexpressible and glorious joy (1 Peter 1:8, NIV).

What is robbing you of your joy today? Can you let it go? Do you need to let go of:

The past?

Worry?

Fear of failure?

Perfectionism?

Unrealistic expectations?

But what if you possessed joy, true joy, in your heart? That *thing* falls into your life and your momentary happiness flees, yet the joy of the Lord continues. Your joy will keep your perspective in balance, allowing you to overcome any temporary un*happiness*.

Turn all of it over to God. He can handle it. Thread your little fingers through His loving fingers and hold on. Then, whoop it up like those shepherds about how you've been granted access to something extraordinary.

Joy is the gigantic secret of the Christian. — G. K. Chesterton

Joy lives in your soul, your heart. It radiates, glows, overpowers. Joy aligns with the hope you hold on to. Thus, it cannot be easily shaken.

Jesus promised joy.

These things I have spoken to you, that my joy may be in you, and that your joy may be full (John 15:11, NIV).

In the verses that precede it, (John 15:1–10), Jesus described his relationship with his Father, using the metaphor of the vine and branches. He assures His disciples that He will remain in them. And, thus, Jesus promised faithful followers that because He will keep His promises, we will have Jesus-filled, joy-filled hearts.

Pray

Father, I pray that You fill me with joy — overwhelming joy. Amen.

Sing

O Holy Night
(Placide Cappeau, 1843)
O holy night, the stars are brightly shining;
it is the night of the dear Savior's birth.
Long lay the world in sin and error pining,
till He appeared and the soul felt its worth.
A thrill of hope, the weary world rejoices,
for yonder breaks a new and glorious morn!

December 13

I HEARD SOMEONE SAY recently that there's no distance God won't go to draw us to Him. While that sounds a bit like an awful line from a contemporary praise song, and it might be... one must ask:

Is there any further distance than to travel from the cosmic realm of God the Father to become a tiny baby born in the most humble setting in an unremarkable town?

So Joseph also went up from the town of Nazareth in Galilee to Judea, to Bethlehem the town of David, because he belonged to the house and line of David. He went there to register with Mary, who was expecting a child. While they were there, the time came for the baby to be born, and she gave birth to her firstborn, a son. She wrapped him in cloths and placed him in a manger (Luke 2:4–7, NIV).

Jesus, the Son of God, enjoyed whatever delights His heavenly home afforded, and gave them up to become flesh on this beautiful, though occasionally dismal, ball circling around the sun.

I hardly think giving up my creature comforts for a week compares to the distance Jesus moved. And yet, I've struggled for a decade to obey God's call to be part of a mission trip in another land. My obedience came to fruition in 2025 when I visited Uganda with a team from my church. I finally "went the distance" in one area of my faith life.

Or maybe distance is a different sort of barrier, a more human one. Perhaps it's preferable to keep Him at arm's length. Then, He might miss that terrible secret on the other side of the door. Or maybe we don't have to worry so much about failing Him if He's far away.

It requires some time to comprehend — to accept — the immensity of God's decision to send His Son far across the vast cosmos He created into a sinful, hopeless world. And of Jesus to submit to making the ultimate sacrifice.

And when we accept Jesus, and quit hiding behind a door and put an end to our fear of failing Him, we can draw closer to Him. Or allow Him to draw us in.

What will you do today to reduce the distance between you and Jesus?

Pray

Dear Jesus, let my desire for a deeper relationship grow. Amen.

Sing

O Come All Ye Faithful
(J.F. Wade, 1841)
O come, all ye faithful, joyful and triumphant,
O come ye, O come ye to Bethlehem!
Come, and behold Him, born the King of angels!
O come, let us adore Him;
O come, let us adore Him;
O come, let us adore Him, Christ, the Lord!

December 14

YOU'D HAVE TO BE pretty hard-hearted not to get slightly sappy around Christmas time. My dear husband, Bob, was a loving, giving man, but he quietly questioned my exuberance for decorating this time of year. I often felt the brakes being applied... oh so subtly.

To be honest, I kept the decorating gas pedal to the floor. Any reduction in decor was based on my schedule or feelings in a given year.

I had typically limited my outdoor decor to a wreath and a few bows here and there. But a few years ago, I got inspired by the crazy tree lighting trend in outdoor decorating—the one that looks a bit like Mardi Gras. To his credit, Bob supported my new outdoor lighting effort. *(I'd finally turned him on to Christmas decor!)* In his last two years of life, I changed the target tree to one he could see from his recliner. He truly loved it.

To be completely fair to Bob and his occasional *grinch*-iness, I could never out-give him on Christmas morning. Giving was certainly his love language. He located some of the most outstanding gifts from unusual places. Items I'd never given a second thought to, but somehow he *knew*. And the jewelry... sigh. Gorgeous things.

He made Christmas morning amazing. But while I have three trees up this season, the floor around them is barren. I miss the excitement of uncovering his surprising gifts.

I miss the love his incredible gifts represented most of all.

As his health declined, Bob joined me in celebrating the love embedded in God's many promises to His children. We watched church services and read through the Psalms, Proverbs, and Luke together. A person of deep spirituality, Bob didn't appreciate "organized religion," but he knew Jesus. So... I get to hold on to, with love, God's promise of eternal life. I'll see my Bob again.

For God so loved the world that he gave his one and only Son, that whoever believes in him shall not perish but have eternal life (John 3:16, NIV).

Pray

Dear Jesus, help me to spread joy as a light in this season. Amen.

Sing

Joyful, Joyful, We Adore Thee
(Henry Van Dyke, 1907)
Joyful, joyful, we adore You,
God of glory, Lord of love;
Hearts unfold like flow'rs before You,
Op'ning to the sun above.
Melt the clouds of sin and sadness;
Drive the dark of doubt away;
Giver of immortal gladness,
Fill us with the light of day!

Week Three Prayer and Scripture Reading

Father in Heaven, thank you for your Son, Jesus, who is the hope and joy of this Christmas season.

Turn my eyes from my problems so that I may find the everlasting joy that a trusting relationship with you can bring me.

As the day of Jesus' birth approaches, calm my heart and mind of my earthly desires for a perfect day and teach me to savor this period of preparation. Amen.

The Word became flesh and made his dwelling among us. We have seen his glory, the glory of the one and only Son, who came from the Father, full of grace and truth (John 1:14, NIV).

December 15

Joy to the world, the Lord is come. These are the opening words of one of my favorite Christmas hymns. Yet Isaac Watts did not write this hymn for his congregation to sing during Advent or on Christmas. He based this song on Psalm 98, where there's not a single mention of Jesus, Mary, or Joseph. Still, one can't help but believe this hymn is perfect for this season.

Shout for joy to the Lord, all the earth, burst into jubilant song with music; make music to the Lord with the harp, with the harp and the sound of singing, with trumpets and the blast of the ram's horn—shout for joy before the Lord, the King (Psalm 98:4-6, NIV).

The prophet Isaiah reflected the psalmist's sentiments.

At that time you will say, Praise the Lord and worship him. Tell everyone what he has done and how great he is. Sing praise to the Lord, because he has done great things. Let all the world know what he has done. Shout and sing for joy, you people of Jerusalem, because the Holy One of Israel does great things before your eyes (Isaiah 12:4–6, NCV).

The third candle in the Advent wreath is rose-pink, the color of joy. It's also called the Shepherd's candle, an homage to those curious shepherds who heard angels on the night Christ was born.

Both Psalm 98 and the Isaiah passage are encouragements to praise and worship our God with everything within us. Praise that can only emanate from a joy-filled heart. After the shepherds left the stable, they told everyone what they had seen, and they glorified God.

They'd just seen the Messiah, and the experience filled them with amazement and joy.

Can't you just imagine those shepherds whooping and praising God? Perhaps the townspeople could hear them all the way from the hillside when they returned to their sheep.

When's the last time you were amazed by God? Does His joy pulse through you? Pause and think about it. That's what this Advent season is for, remember — to slow us down.

Stop and be amazed. Feel His joy.

Pray

God of Heaven, give me faith to live joyfully as I wait for your promises to be fulfilled. Amen.

Sing

Joy to the World!
(Isaac Watts, 1754)
Joy to the world, the Lord is come!
Let earth receive her King;
let ev'ry heart prepare him room,
and heav'n and nature sing,
and heav'n and nature sing,
and heav'n and nature sing.

December 16

LIKE MANY PEOPLE, I have a definitive list of songs that make me switch the radio station. At Christmas time, those are mainly secular songs about holly-jolly days and red-nosed creatures.

A few decades ago, I fell in love with a sweet book series set in the fictional town of Mitford, North Carolina. There, the chubby Episcopal priest, Father Tim, struggled to fit into the community and into his priestly frock. He ministered to some fine people.

Father Tim's favorite Christmas song was "In the Bleak Midwinter," which I had never heard of. Being a bit musically inclined, I looked it up and fell in love with the lyrics. My church choir sang it one year in our Christmas program, and I was so moved, I could barely croak out the last stanza's lyrics.

Christina Rossetti submitted this poem to a magazine in 1872, but it wasn't set to music until 1906 by Gustav Holst, 12 years after her death. It captures not only the homage that one should pay to the newborn King, but also the struggle to find a suitable birthday gift for Him.

My son, give me your heart and let your eyes delight in my ways (Proverbs 23:26, NIV).

I love this song because it evokes the loneliness and barrenness of Christ's birth in the harsh setting of a stable or cave. Not fit for a newborn baby, and certainly not suitable for the King of Heaven.

And we know from Gospel accounts that Jesus never got the proper welcome that was His due.

I love those who love me, and those who seek me find me (Proverbs 8:17, NIV).

Rosetti's inspired words remind me of what God requires of me every day: ***give Him my heart.***

What do this song's lyrics mean to you? Can you croak out a prayer to give Him your heart, your life, and all that is within you?

Pray

Father, in the quiet of each day, help me seek You first. Amen.

Sing

In the Bleak Midwinter
(Rossetti, 1872)
Our God, heaven cannot hold him, nor earth sustain;
heaven and earth shall flee away when he comes to reign:
in the bleak midwinter a stable place sufficed
the Lord God Almighty, Jesus Christ.
What can I give Him, Poor as I am?
If I were a shepherd, I would bring a lamb.
If I were a wise man, I would do my part.
Yet what I can I give him — Give my heart.

December 17

We approach the Christmas season with a sense of hopefulness. Mothers hope their children go to bed early on Christmas Eve. Husbands hope their team wins a bowl game. Families hope everyone behaves, for a change.

When I was younger, I hoped for a doll or a bicycle. I had reasonable wishes, so my hopes were seldom dashed by my parents.

Since my husband of only 13 years passed away, I've been digging through his many spaces around our home — garages, closets, and a few cabinets I seldom peeked inside. Finally reaching the back of one garage bay, I found a locked cabinet in mid-century modern style. The bottom of the doors were water damaged, so I wasn't overly concerned about how to get into it quietly, if you know what I mean.

It was so heavy, I was certain it held a prize or two. So, on Thanksgiving afternoon, my mum, my daughter, and I stood in hopeful anticipation while the daughter's fellow pried it open. He was excited just to perform the destructive task! Our hopes were dashed soundly. The contents included rolled-up carpeting, a ghastly green bedding set, and two ceiling fan motors. Being grownups, we had a good giggle. The cabinet quickly faded as we chatted around the dining table again.

I'm so glad I had no serious hopes pinned to that cabinet's contents. I try to keep a hopeful posture mostly, and I know my faith has much to do with that. Even in my grief, I remain hopeful.

God's Word offers so much hope. The prophet Isaiah poured out many assurances of a world where everyone will experience hope and peace.

You will keep in perfect peace those whose minds are steadfast, because they trust in you (Isaiah 2:3–5, NIV).

Christ Jesus, too, offered words of encouragement about a new day when He will return with the clouds.

"Always be ready, because you don't know the day your Lord will come" (Matthew 24:42, NCV).

So, no matter how many times your daily wishes don't come true, He's still holding your hand and leading you where He wants you to be.

Pray

Jesus, You are my hope—steady, certain, and true. Amen.

Sing

It Came Upon a Midnight Clear
(Edmund Sears, 1849)
It came upon the midnight clear,
that glorious song of old,
from angels bending near the earth
to touch their harps of gold:
"Peace on the earth, good will to men,
from heaven's all-gracious King."

December 18

BEING BUSY IS A prison for the overachiever, the perfectionist, the one who's trying to escape whatever. While busy-ness may feel like a success strategy in the short-term, the long-term losses are real.

You definitely lose when:

- You miss that gorgeous sunset on your drive home because you're arranging a playdate for your over-scheduled child.

- While texting, you miss your friend's facial expression as she opens your special gift.

- You're late for a child's school production.

You've probably heard that the Hebrew word "shalom" means peace. But it means far more than that — whole, safe, or sound. It denotes a life well-lived, one's *best life.*

Wouldn't you like *that* kind of peace? We should be seeking peace *with* God, the peace *from* God, and the peace we gain *from knowing God* through His word.

Now may the Lord of peace give you peace at all times and in every way. The Lord be with all of you (2 Thessalonians 3:16, NCV).

There's not a day goes by that most of us don't wish for world peace. Jesus tempered those hopes with a more realistic view:

You will hear of wars and rumors of wars, but see to it that you are not alarmed. Such things must happen, but the end is still to come. Nation will rise against nation, and kingdom against kingdom. All these are the beginning of birth pains (Matthew 24:6–8, NIV).

But one day, as the prophet Isaiah announced, there will be peace when "the earth is full of the knowledge of the Lord" (Isaiah 11:9). Let us be that knowledge and fill our immediate worlds with the things of God today.

And in the quiet... in the waiting and expectation of this Advent season, we can pull God's peace into our hearts.

Perhaps you should pause — ask for His peace now.

Pray

Father, breathe peace into my soul when chaos surrounds me. Amen.

Sing

Silent Night
(Joseph Mohr, 1818)
Silent night, holy night,
All is calm, all is bright
Round yon virgin mother and child!
Holy Infant so tender and mild,
Sleep in heavenly peace,
Sleep in heavenly peace.

December 19

HUMANS HAVE ALWAYS SOUGHT peace. We seek it for our own heart, for our friends and family, and for the world. We seek calming peace to replace anxiety about finances, relationships, politics, and so much more. The world is filled with anxiety-producing elements and events.

By meditating on God's word, however, we can grow closer to Him and realize His peace. It's one of the best rewards of being a Christ-follower.

The personal pursuit of peace is important. A peaceful mind is able to focus on the good all around. God wants us to have peace, and in turn, He expects us to be peacemakers.

Before Christ was born, God had made countless promises of a Savior, a Messiah. They're scattered throughout the Old Testament.

Jesus, as well, foretold His resurrection, transformation, and ultimate return. These promises demonstrate God's interest in our personal peace. Knowing that He is going to do what He has said should give the believer peace beyond measure. Things *are* going to work out for good—in His timing, of course.

His peace is coming. World peace seems unattainable most days. There's so much hate and terror in the world. But God has promised the end of war — no more nations set against each other. Nations will willingly lay down their implements of death.

God exhorts us to be still, to cease striving, to draw peace into our hearts. He keeps His word, and the world will one day bow down before Him. What a promise!

Be still, and know that I am God; I will be exalted among the nations, I will be exalted in the earth (Psalm 46:10, NIV).

I simply adore the work of Handel in his oratoria called *Messiah*. The scriptures set to music are perfectly chosen, and the music is divine. I urge you to listen to it. I dare you to walk away unmoved.

Comfort, comfort my people, says your God. Speak tenderly to Jerusalem, and cry to her that her warfare is ended, that her iniquity is pardoned, that she has received from the LORD's hand double for all her sins. A voice cries: "In the wilderness prepare the way of the LORD; make straight in the desert a highway for our God. Every valley shall be lifted up, and every mountain and hill be made low; the uneven ground shall become level, and the rough places a plain (Isaiah 40:1–4, ESV).

Pray

Jesus, empty my heart of worries and fill it with Your peace. Amen.

Sing

Comfort Ye
(G.F. Handel, 1741)
Comfort ye
Comfort ye my people
Comfort ye
Comfort ye my people
Saith your God
Saith your God.

December 20

THERE IS SOMETHING QUITE spectacular about holding a newborn baby. An infant offers a sweetness, an effervescence that's indescribable. A baby gives us a special feeling in our hearts. Imagine kissing the face of God — that glorified experience Mary and Joseph actually had every day.

At Christmas time, we feel the specialness a baby brings to the moment. But Jesus isn't a baby anymore. We merely celebrate His birth at this time of year. Yet... I wonder about a few things. I'm a bit like that skeptical disciple, Thomas.

Not long ago, someone gave me the book *Gentle and Lowly*. Its subtitle is *The Heart of Christ for Sinners and Sufferers*. The book focuses entirely on the heart of Jesus. The author sifts through scripture and other writings about Jesus by famous theologians.

I'm sort of embarrassed. Ashamed that I've been a believer for decades, yet I've never clearly understood the gravitas that is mine because I am His sister. A close, tightly knit family with Jesus has been offered, and I've been gazing elsewhere.

While reading that book, my heart overflowed with a strange joy, and simultaneously despaired of the things I have missed. My faith life, nay my entire life, could have been so different had I felt His ear bent to my lips, waiting for me to give voice to the hurt and pain that's so common in our human existence. He was ready, right there, to hear my disgraced confessions and the groanings of my broken heart.

Consider this and tell me if I'm way off-base... The baby Jesus is approachable: a sweet angelic child swaddled and living in a stable surrounded by sheep and cattle. The Christmas vision of our Lord. But the suffering Savior, somehow He's aloof, up in heaven with the Father. That's what we tell ourselves. We talk of "Jesus living in my heart," but most often we beckon Him to *come down* from heaven to help us out. Don't we?

Or maybe it's just me who missed the memo about the true heart of Jesus, our perfect Brother who looks out for us. As Dane Ortland writes,

He isn't like you. Even the most intense of human love is but the faintest echo of heaven's cascading abundance (p. 160).

You snuggled with the baby Jesus over the past few weeks. Isn't it time to hold out your arms and your heart to the Risen Savior and let Him hold you now?

Pray

Dear Jesus, let joy rise up in me because of who You are. Amen.

Sing

What Child Is This?
(W. Chatterton Dix, 1861)
What Child is this, who, laid to rest,
On Mary's lap is sleeping?
Whom angels greet with anthems sweet,
While shepherds watch are keeping?

December 29

I LOVE CHRISTMAS. I mean, I love-love it. As the song says, it's the most wonderful time of the year. I love the colors, the aromas, the lights. I love the music too. Most of all, I love the reason for the season: Jesus' birth. God's love was born in human form that special night.

The first thing I do when I begin decorating my house for Christmas is put out my Nativity set. It's a new-ish one, and I've received new pieces like sheep and an angel the past few years. It now fills my entire kitchen fireplace mantel. When my kids were young, it was important they understand that Christmas is about Jesus, not Santa. We had a small nativity set with a twiggy shelter and porcelain figurines. Because the word "nativity" was hard to remember, they called it "the Jesus thing" and were always excited to help with its setup.

Honestly, I feel more loving toward others at this time of year. I don't know if that's a good thing or not — shouldn't I feel the same all year? Maybe it's the gift-buying, which I enjoy doing. You know, thinking about a loved one and what a perfect gift for them might be triggers genuinely warm and deeper feelings of love.

When the angel told Mary that she would conceive and deliver God's perfect son, here's what happened.

And Mary said: My soul glorifies the Lord and my spirit rejoices in God my Savior, for he has been mindful of the humble state of his servant. From now on all generations will call me blessed, for the Mighty

One has done great things for me — holy is his name (Luke 1:46–49, NIV).

In that moment, she worshipped and honored God for choosing her. She was blessed, and she felt loved.

Imagine. You're Mary, chosen to give birth to God's son. You'll name him Jesus.

One of my favorite contemporary Christmas songs is *Mary, Did You Know?* written by Mark Lowry and Buddy Green. In it, Mary is asked if she realized that she was carrying a healer, a deliverer, a miracle worker, a ruler, a perfect sacrificial lamb.

Imagine. You're Mary, kissing the cheek of your sweet baby boy. Kissing the face of God.

Mary surely knew Who she cradled in her arms. Do you know Him too?

Pray

Father, thank you for sending Your Son to offer salvation to all who accept it. Amen.

Sing

The Lord's Prayer
Luke 11:2-4
Our Father, which art in heaven,
Hallowed be Thy name.
Thy kingdom come, Thy will be done
on earth as it is in heaven.
Give us this day our daily bread,
and forgive us our debts,
as we forgive our debtors.

Week Four Prayer & Scripture Reading

Gracious God, as Christmas draws near, prepare my heart to receive the Christ child.
In these final days of waiting, may my home become a sanctuary of peace.
Kindle within me the flame of expectation and joy.
Transform my hurried preparations into acts of worship, my gift-giving into expressions of grace.
Help me remember that while I busy myself with earthly celebrations, You

are still writing Your story
of redemption across this
broken world.
Come, Emmanuel.
Amen.

*For to us a child is born, to us a son is given, and the government will be on his shoulders. And he will be called Wonderful Counselor, Mighty God, Everlasting Father, Prince of Peace. Of the greatness of his government and peace there will be no end. He will reign on David's throne and over his kingdom, establishing and upholding it with justice and righteousness from that time on and forever. The zeal of the LORD Almighty will accomplish this (*Isaiah 9:6-7, *NIV).*

December 22

THE FOURTH CANDLE IN the Advent wreath is purple. It's sometimes called the Angel's Candle. Earlier in this waiting season, we witnessed the shepherd's overwhelming joy after they heard the angel and visited the newborn Christ-child.

Let's spend a little more time meditating on the peace of the Messiah. What does it look like in action?

He will stand and shepherd his flock in the strength of the Lord, in the majesty of the name of the Lord his God. And they will live securely, for then his greatness will reach to the ends of the earth. And he will be our peace (Micah 5:4–5, NIV).

When we think of what peace means today, what likely comes to mind first is the "lack of war and conflict." A mother may mutter under her breath that she'd just like some momentary peace from her needy family. She doesn't really *need* a beach chair and a week of silence (though it might be nice).

Would you like a quiet minute alone?

The holidays can be most unpeaceful. But we make them that way, don't we? Busy, busy — rushing to kids' events and parties, shopping at the mall, rummaging through the pantry for a missing cookie ingredient. We make this a fractious time. It's so unnecessary.

How can you usher peace into your life today? What about infusing peace into the life of another? Could you ease a family's worry? Remove the pall of earthly concerns for one day for someone?

How about these ideas for a start:

- Spend more time in personal devotions

- Run an errand for an overburdened friend

- Provide a meal for someone

- Give to or volunteer at a food bank

- Get a group together to sing carols at a nursing home.

Isn't Advent the perfect time to pursue peace in your life and your community?

Pray

Heavenly father, may the Prince of Peace reign in my home and in my heart. Amen.

Sing

God Rest You Merry, Gentlemen
(English carol, 1760)
God rest you merry, gentlemen,
let nothing you dismay,
remember Christ our Savior
was born on Christmas Day
to save us all from Satan's pow'r
when we were gone astray.
O tidings of comfort and joy.

December 23

Do you ever fret about what to buy someone? Birthdays, Christmas, special days — they come, they go, yet the mystery of 'what to buy' remains.

A recent sermon spurred me to read John 15 as soon as I arrived home. Hearing my pastor speak of it, I was inspired by the idea of remaining in His love and how it relates to gift-giving.

As the Father has loved me, so have I loved you. Now remain in my love. If you keep my commands, you will remain in my love, just as I have kept my Father's commands and remain in his love (John 15:9–10, NIV).

It's not a secret that most people we love would prefer to enjoy simple moments with us. Our parents and grandparents rarely have a need for things. What they wish for most is time... time with family and friends. Sometimes, a phone call will suffice. A surprise card in the mail tells someone you're with them in spirit.

When we remain in God's divine presence, we can more easily share ourselves and His love. The quietness of remaining in His love makes me feel a bit warm and fuzzy. To be still and know, for example... there's incredible power in remaining in that place with God. Being present.

Presence.

Can you give the gift of your presence to someone today? Maybe it's not a family member who needs you, but someone else. God will not ignore the loving gift of your time and attention to someone who needs to be seen and heard.

And do not forget to do good and to share with others, for with such sacrifices God is pleased.

That presence means you won't be fretting about what to buy, and it will usher in peace and joy.

It's a holy thing. Holy indeed.

Pray

Let my heart be quick to respond to Your voice, Lord. Amen.

Sing

Take My Life, And Let It Be
(Francis Havergal, 1874)
Take my life and let it be
consecrated, Lord, to thee.
Take my moments and my days;
Take my hands and let them move
at the impulse of thy love.
Take my feet and let them be
swift and beautiful for thee.

December 24

Do you love Christmas? I mean, *really love* Christmas. I'm nuts about the music and the decorations. Oh, and the children's pageants. Just everything.

I can get excited about Christmas as early as July. But as my neighbor says when someone complains about the swiftness of time, "next thing you know, it's Christmas!" He's right... this incredible season really is always right around the corner.

And then there's the manger with the Madonna, Joseph, and the Christ Child — the reason for the season, as we say.

Jesus... The Prince of Peace.

The angels promised peace on earth when they sang to the shepherds in the fields.

Glory to God in the highest, and on earth peace, and goodwill toward men! (Luke 2:14, NIV).

But in contrast, Jesus said,

Do not suppose that I have come to bring peace to the earth. I did not come to bring peace, but a sword (Matthew 10:34, NIV).

Can we reconcile those two scriptures? Perhaps this will help: Jesus came to earth to establish a path of peace between humans and God — a path fraught with challenges we create. Jesus brings peace today to those who believe. Ultimately, Jesus will bring peace in its fullest to the earth when all things on Earth as we know it pass away.

For unto us a Child is born, unto us a Son is given; and the government shall be upon His shoulder. And His name shall be called Wonderful, Counselor, The Mighty God, The Everlasting Father, The Prince of Peace (Isaiah 9:6, KJV).

Can you even read that verse without singing it? Handel captured this verse in *Messiah* so well, you have to hear it — as I've already told you.

Do you experience peace every day? Even in the midst of anxiety or mayhem, you can still find peace. In Him. Jesus, the Prince of Peace.

Pray

God of peace, calm my anxious thoughts and still my racing heart.
Amen.

Sing

When I Survey the Wondrous Cross
(Isaac Watts, 1707)
When I survey the wondrous cross
On which the Prince of glory died,
My richest gain I count but loss,
And pour contempt on all my pride.

December 25

Merry Christmas!

The Advent period (the time of waiting and anticipation) ends with the birth of Jesus, of course. No more waiting. Jesus is born!

We have journeyed together in this Advent season through texts about hope, love, peace, obedience. And a bit more, right?

Christmastide, also known as the twelve days of Christmas, runs from December 25 until January 6. Or from sundown December 24 until January 5, depending on your liturgical leanings. Most of us treat these days as a period of reflection, mainly because a new year is approaching. We do like to crowd out the present season with the next one on the calendar, don't we?

But let's talk about this idea of reflection. Do you reflect? Do you engage in anxious meanderings or maybe serious contemplation?

What do you usually think about during Christmas time? Today is Christmas Day, and your hours may not be your own for a good part of it, but remember these promises:

Because of Jesus, we can be made new.

He who was seated on the throne said, "I am making everything new!" Then he said, "Write this down, for these words are trustworthy and true" (Revelation 21:5, NIV).

Because of Jesus, we can praise.

Lord, our Lord, how majestic is your name in all the earth! You have set your glory in the heavens (Psalm 8:1, NIV).

Because of Jesus, we can access wisdom.

But the wisdom that comes from heaven is first of all pure; then peace-loving, considerate, submissive, full of mercy and good fruit, impartial and sincere (James 3:17, NIV).

Because of Jesus, you don't have to worry about how you "measure up" in this world. You can live in certainty of your value, your worth. You can go into a new day, a new year with the hope, peace, joy, and love only He can sustain.

I pray you can find some quiet time today to reflect, to praise, to be made new.

Forget the former things; do not dwell on the past. See, I am doing a new thing! Now it springs up; do you not perceive it? I am making a way in the wilderness and streams in the wasteland (Isaiah 43:18-19, NIV).

Pray

Jesus, thank You for coming in human form to save us. Amen.

Sing

Praise, My Soul, the King of Heaven
(Henry F. Lyte, 1834)
Fatherlike He tends and spares us
Well our feeble frame he knows
In His hand He gently bears us
Rescues us from all our foes.

December 26

THE 400 YEARS OF silence refer to the period between the Old Testament and New Testament, during which, it is believed God did not speak — no Scripture was written.

The Old Testament books may not be ordered in today's Bible as they were written, but the gap between the Old and New Testaments is real. The Apocrypha was likely written in the four centuries between Old and New Testament works, but their inspiration has been questioned over the last 200 years.

Prophets offered inspired warnings about the coming quiet and its effect on the people. So we are left with 400 years of God's silence.

"The days are coming," declares the Sovereign Lord, "when I will send a famine through the land — not a famine of food or a thirst for water, but a famine of hearing the words of the Lord. People will stagger from sea to sea and wander from north to east, searching for the word of the Lord, but they will not find it" (Amos 8:11-12, NIV).

Between the time of Malachi and the Messiah's arrival, prophecies were fulfilled, such as the 2,300 days of desecration between 171 and 165 B.C. found in Daniel 8:14. Unfortunately, the Hebrew people did not study scripture or consider the prophesy fulfillment to seek God during this time of silence. As God was obviously doing, they, too, should have been preparing for the Messiah. But they were so lost and separated from God's words, most of the Jews could not even consider the concept of a humble Messiah, born as a baby.

Rejoice greatly, O daughter of Zion! Shout aloud, O daughter of Jerusalem! Behold, your king is coming to you; righteous and having salvation is he, humble and mounted on a donkey, on a colt, the foal of a donkey (Zechariah 9:9, ESV).

If God had finished His work of revelation at that time, then God was surely preparing to rescue His people. Preparing, in fact, the way for Jesus' birth and ministry.

We could say, now even, that we are now in a 2,000–year silence. But we *know* the Messiah is Jesus... and that he is coming back.

A second advent.

Praise God!

Pray

Even so, come Lord Jesus! Amen.

Sing

Christ is Coming!
(John R. MacDuff, 1853)
Christ is coming! Let creation
from her groans and travail cease;
let the glorious proclamation
hope restore and faith increase:
Christ is coming! Christ is coming!
Come, Thou blessed Prince of Peace,
come, Thou blessed Prince of Peace.

December 27

I HAVE A VIVID imagination. But I am always astounded and a little envious of creative people who produce material that captures the hearts of millions. Take, for example, John Newton, who penned the words of probably the most well-known song in the world, "Amazing Grace."

For from his fullness we have all received, grace upon grace (John 1:16, ESV).

In Newton's time, the slave trade was an enormous segment of the economy. To fight against that tide would have been an astronomical burden. Yet, Newton fought. He knew it was the proper thing for him to do.

Today, the world outside our windows is in chaos. Nothing seems stable — not our money system, the employment world, or our social structure. It's requiring more and more effort for us not to worry about the giant tears in our social fabric. And what that means for the future, a future I hope will be certain and unshakeable for my children and the next generation.

And then I have my own chaos. I lost my husband to cancer. Settling his estate was difficult, and it took a long time to see light at the end of that messy tunnel. Then, I see the signs that my best company, my darling dogs, are aging. Family members are mired in their own difficulties — things I can only stand by and observe.

But unlike Newton, I can't really fight any of the problems of this world. I am able, though, to surrender my cares to the Lord. You can too.

He'll bring us through them. Even though we may be swept off our feet by terrible tides, our Lord and Savior can do far beyond what we can imagine. He can return us safely to shore.

Now to him who is able to do immeasurably more than all we ask or imagine, according to his power that is at work within us (Ephesians 3:20, NIV).

Pray

Heavenly Father, even in chaotic times, may I hear Your whisper and feel Your presence. Amen.

Sing

Amazing Grace
(John Newton, 1779)
Through many dangers, toils, and snares,
I have already come.
Tis grace that brought me safe thus far.
And grace will lead me home.

December 28

BACK IN THE DAY, I was pretty good at memorizing scripture. My college roommates and I devoted one semester to committing Philippians 4 to memory (23 verses!). We practiced together every Wednesday night during our devotion time. Independent work was required the rest of the week even though we were also studying for tests, doing homework, and pondering the silly things freshman girls were bound to fret over.

I'm not very good at it anymore. I blame it on my age. Maybe a lack of desire too. But I have this weird fantasy of being imprisoned and wishing I could recite God's word as I while away the days behind bars. Do you think that's odd? I agree, it's a little weird.

I'm fairly certain that a Sunday school teacher made such a case for learning scripture with his skeptical students. Somehow, *that's* what stuck with me.

However, I think I have a respectable canon of verses that could keep me focused on my faith if I'm ever in adverse circumstances. I wish I had more stored away, though. Indeed, one scripture that speaks to this important practice is Psalm 119:11.

The version that has been indelibly inscribed on my heart for decades is from the King James:

Thy word have I hid in mine heart, that I might not sin against thee (Psalm 119:11, KJV).

I'm forever grateful to the Sunday school teachers who devoted themselves to my discipleship. Today, I can write about my faith and the lessons God's Word brings forth because they chiseled biblical concepts on my young and receptive heart.

Reflecting on your Bible study, have you hid His word in your heart? Can you do better in the new year?

Pray

Lord, may I rejoice in Your goodness today and every day. Amen.

Sing

Wonderful Words of Life
(Phillip P. Bliss, 1874)
Sing them over again to me,
wonderful words of life;
let me more of their beauty see,
wonderful words of life;
words of life and beauty,
teach me faith and duty.

December 29

WE LIVE OUR DAYS at breakneck speed. *Faster is better* — a significant theme of the past century. We find ourselves slaves to *hurry*, and to the technology meant to save us time.

Upon the invention of that technological freak, the sundial, Plautus angrily wrote, *The gods confound the man who first found out how to distinguish hours! Confound him, too. Who in this place set up a sun-dial? To cut and hack my days so wretchedly into small portions!*

Chunks of available time seem perfect. Then, we use those morsels of time to plot out our days and hours. Sadly, we love a full grid. We have no free time, for when any free moments miraculously appear, they leak between our fingers. Or more likely, we capture them in a net of yet more busyness.

For the Jesus follower, the unsettled world and our own frenetic pace give us reason to cry out, Even so, Lord Jesus, come! This is not how we're meant to live.

Jesus didn't scurry about, and aren't we meant to strive to be more like Him? How can we hear His voice when the *whoosh* of deadlines flying past drowns Him out?

In his book, *The Ruthless Elimination of Hurry*, John Mark Comer asks, is an overbusy, digitally distracted life the greatest threat to spiritual life? It has been so in my past. How about in your life?

The prophet Habakkuk started out whining that God didn't make any sense. But as God's vision unfolded before him, the prophet learned.

For still the vision awaits its appointed time; it hastens to the end — it will not lie. If it seems slow, wait for it; it will surely come; it will not delay (Habakkuk 2:3, ESV).

Who originally said, "*Anything worth having is worth waiting for?*" I couldn't figure that out, so my mom gets the credit.

Wait. Slow down. While these words have little currency in our culture, they mean something to me. Like Habakkuk, I want my waiting and listening to become a prayer.

I will rejoice in the Lord; *I will be joyful in God, my Savior (Habakkuk 3:18, NIV).*

Pray

Help me, God, to find peace in the pause. Amen.

Sing

Be Thou My Vision
(Eleanor Hull, 1905)
Be thou my vision, O Lord of my heart;
Naught be all else to me save that thou art.
Thou my best thought by day and by night;
Waking or sleeping, thy presence my light.

December 30

O LORD, YOU HAVE searched me and known me! You know when I sit down and when I rise up; you discern my thoughts from afar (Psalm 139:1–2, ESV).

One could make a year-long study of Psalm 139 alone, for there we find the omniscient God, who knows everything. David describes God's intimate knowledge so beautifully in those 24 verses. It is an awe-inspiring psalm about our Maker.

Still, those first two verses hit the highlights, don't they?

God's foreknowledge. His love. God's creation. His protection.

I want this God.

Yes, yes, I know. I already have this God in my life, but the ball is in my court, so to speak, to bring Him, knit Him, into my every moment.

I know, I know. He's *already there* in those moments. Yet sadly, I find myself too busy to see and hear Him. Even when I crave His nearness, my mind is foolishly diverted by minutiae.

And it's when I am buried in the trivialities of life, I forget God knows best. I can turn over all worry and uncertainty to Him.

I need that God. Every day. That God, that inescapable God, is here in the now. But in my humanity, I cannot keep Him close enough.

It's up to me — and you — to invite Him into the midst of messy everyday moments and ask for help or peace or hope. Or whatever the circumstance requires — He can fill the need. He's holding the bag with the goods we desire because He already knows.

Pray

Restore my hope, Lord, when the world feels dim. Amen.

Sing

I Need Thee Every Hour
(Hawks & Lowry, 1872)
I need Thee ev'ry hour, most gracious Lord;
no tender voice like Thine can peace afford.
I need Thee, O I need Thee; ev'ry hour I need Thee;
O bless me now, my Savior, I come to Thee.

December 31

YOU KNOW WHAT I'D like to do one morning? Wake up with my focus immediately and entirely on God. This issue has been weighing on me for quite a while. The other morning, I woke early and had some time to be still and prevent my mind from slipping into the 100-mph mode it's accustomed to. It worked for about five minutes.

In that short time, I prayed and asked God for this very blessing, an undivided heart, a heart that sought only Him. Praying scripture to God is good for us, so this was my prayer:

Create in me a pure heart, O God, and renew a steadfast spirit within me (Psalm 51:10, NIV).

David was an amazing monitor of his heart. I try to be like David, but I have a busy life, you know?

We were designed with a pure heart, but sin entered the Garden of Eden and now humans have two natures: the God-seeking and the sin-seeking. Ezekiel called the sinful one a heart of stone.

Teach me your way, Lord, that I may rely on your faithfulness; give me an undivided heart, that I may fear your name (Psalm 86:11, NIV).

So how do we get an undivided heart? How do we even get to the point of "relying on his faithfulness"?

Be S-T-I-L-L

· **S**tudy His word

· **T**alk to Him

· **I**nspire others with His stories

· **L**earn your weaknesses so you can address them
· **L**isten to the whisperings of the Holy Spirit

Brothers and sisters, I do not consider myself yet to have taken hold of it. But one thing I do: Forgetting what is behind and straining toward what is ahead, I press on toward the goal to win the prize for which God has called me heavenward in Christ Jesus (Philippians 3:13, NIV).

This scripture gives me hope. If even Paul was still seeking God's transforming work in his life, there's hope for me! My hope for your new year is that you'll "be still" in the moment, and move closer to a heart for God.

Pray

Dear Jesus, as I enter a new year, help me love as You love—with grace and kindness. Amen.

Sing

I Am Resolved
(Palmer Hartsough, 1893)
I am resolved no longer to linger,
charmed by the world's delight;
things that are higher, things that are nobler,
these have allured my sight.

Prayer for the New Year & Scripture Reading

Faithful God, I stand at the threshold of a new year, with a heart full of expectation. You have been my constant companion through every season past, and I trust in Your unwavering faithfulness for the days ahead. Grant me the courage to embrace the unknown with hope, wisdom to discern Your will in each decision, and strength to walk faithfully in Your ways. Help me remember that Your mercies are new every morning, Your love never failing. As I write new chapters in my story, may they reflect Your grace and goodness. Lead me forward with confidence, knowing that You who began a good work in me will be faithful to complete it. Amen.

But those who hope in the Lord will renew their strength. They will soar on wings like eagles; they will run and not grow weary, they will walk and not be faint (Isaiah 40:31, NIV).

Citation Page

Lewis, C. S. 2012. Mere Christianity. London, England: William Collins.

Ortlund, Dane Calvin. 2020. Gentle and Lowly: The Heart of Christ for Sinners and Sufferers. Wheaton: Crossway. Used with permission.

Scripture quotations taken from the ESV® Bible (The Holy Bible, English Standard Version®), copyright© 2001 by Crossway Bibles, a publishing ministry of Good News Publishers. Used by permission. All rights reserved.

Scripture quotations taken from the Holy Bible, New International Version ®, NIV ® Copyright © 1973, 1978, 1984, 2011 by Biblica, Inc. Used with permission. All rights reserved worldwide.

Scripture quotations taken from the New Century Version®. Copyright © 2005 by Thomas Nelson. Used by permission. All rights reserved.

Scripture quotations taken from the Authorized (King James) Version, public domain.

All song quotations are from Hymnary.org website and special contents copyright 2007-present. Harry Plantinga.

About the author

JULIE IS A WIDOW, a mom, a daughter, a sister, and a friend. She's also the daughter of the one true King. Her faith keeps her going every day.

Julie retired from college administration in 2020 and embarked on a writing career. She publishes essays on Medium.com and Substack on a variety of topics. She's also published three fiction novels under the name J. J. Ranson.

Novels by J. J. Ranson

She Danced Anyway
His Christmas Muse
Her Christmas Project

www.ingramcontent.com/pod-product-compliance
Lightning Source LLC
Chambersburg PA
CBHW051643120626
46551CB00015B/2194